Tell Me Again
How the White Heron Rises
and Flies Across the Nacreous River
at Twilight
Toward the Distant Islands

Other Books by Hayden Carruth

POETRY
  The Crow and the Heart
  Journey to a Known Place
  The Norfolk Poems
  North Winter
  Nothing for Tigers
  Contra Mortem
  The Clay Hill Anthology
  For You
  From Snow and Rock, from Chaos
  Dark World
  The Bloomingdale Papers
  Loneliness
  Aura
  Brothers, I Loved You All
  The Mythology of Dark and Light
  The Sleeping Beauty
  If You Call This Cry a Song
  Asphalt Georgics
  The Oldest Killed Lake in North America
  Lighter Than Air Craft
  Mother
  The Selected Poetry of Hayden Carruth

FICTION
  Appendix A

CRITICISM
  After the Stranger
  Working Papers
  Effluences from the Sacred Caves
  Sitting In

ANTHOLOGIES
  The Voice That Is Great Within Us
  The Bird/Poem Book

HAYDEN CARRUTH

Tell Me Again
How the White Heron Rises
and Flies Across the Nacreous River
at Twilight
Toward the Distant Islands

A NEW DIRECTIONS BOOK

Grateful acknowledgment is made to the editors and publishers of chapbooks, periodicals, and limited editions in which these poems first appeared: *The Breadloaf Anthology of Contemporary American Poetry, The Chowder Review, Country Journal, Ironwood, New Directions in Prose and Poetry 49, New England Review/Bread Loaf Quarterly, Paris Review, Poetry East, Ploughshares, The Southern California Anthology, The Southern Review, Sulfur, Tri-Quarterly, The Virginia Quarterly Review.* The poem "Mother" was first published in *The Sewanee Review* and then as a chapbook in a limited edition by Allen Hoey at The Tamarack Press in 1985. Somewhat more than half these poems were published in a limited edition, *Lighter Than Air Craft,* by Mary Chenoweth and Barnard Taylor at The Press of Appletree Alley, Lewisburg, Pennsylvania, in 1985.

Manufactured in the United States of America.
New Directions Books are printed on acid-free paper.
Published simultaneously in Canada by Penguin Books Canada Limited.
First published as New Directions Paperbook 677 in 1989.

Library of Congress Cataloging-in-Publication Data
Carruth, Hayden, 1921–
    Tell me again how the white heron rises and flies across the nacreous river at twilight toward the distant islands / Hayden Carruth.
        p. cm. — (A New Directions paperbook : 677)
    Includes index.
    ISBN 0–8112–1104–5 (alk. paper)
    I. Title.
PS3505.A77594T45   1989
811'.54—dc20
                                                        89–31603
                                                        CIP

New Directions Books are published for James Laughlin
by New Directions Publishing Corporation,
80 Eighth Avenue, New York 10011

THIRD PRINTING

For GALWAY KINNELL

CONTENTS

Tell Me Again
How the White Heron Rises
and Flies Across the Nacreous River
at Twilight
Toward the Distant Islands

I

The Incorrigible Dirigible

Never in any circumstances think you can tell the men from the
　　boys. Or the sheep from the goats.
Nevertheless unavoidably and interminably—up to a point!—one
　　observes tendencies, the calculus
Of discriminative factors in human affairs. Alcoholism, for instance,
　　is the "occupational disease of writers"
(And a good fat multitone in vox populi too, that sad song), and I
　　cannot but approve
My friends Ray Carver and John Cheever, who conquered it in
　　themselves;
I cannot help, for that matter and to the extent I am friendly with
　　myself at all,
Approving my own reformation, which began 30 years ago today,
　　the 3rd September 1953.
Ah, your genuine lush never forgets the date of his last one, believe
　　me, whether yesterday or yesteryear (*le trente-troisième de
　　mon eage*),
And one time I asked John, who had quit at 65, why he bothered.
　　　　"At your age I think I'd have gone on out loaded," I said.
"Puking all over someone else's furniture?" he answered, and much
　　can be derived
From his typical compression of judgment. We were men as men
　　go, drinking coffee and squinting through cigarette smoke
Where we sat at a zinc-topped table at 7 o'clock in the morning.
We were men buoyant in cynicism.
Now I remember Lucinda de Ciella who drank a pony of Strega
　　every morning before breakfast

And was sober and beautiful for ninety years, I remember her
	saying how peaceful
Were the Atlantic crossings by dirigible in the 1930's when her
	husband was Ecuadorian ambassador to Bruxelles.
Such a magnificent, polychronogeneous idea, flight by craft that
	are lighter than air!
I am sure it will be revived.

Not Transhistorical Death, or at Least Not Quite

Jim Wright who was a good poet and my friend, died two or three
      years ago.
I was told at the time that we did not lose him.
I was told that memories of him would keep him in this world.
I don't remember who told me this, just that it was in the air, like
      the usual fall-out from funerals.

I knew it was wrong.
Now I have begun to think how it was wrong.
I have begun to see that it was not only sentimental but simplistic.
I have examined Jim in my mind.
I remember him, but the memories are as dead as he is.
What is more important is how I see him now.
There, there, in that extreme wide place, that emptiness.
He is near enough to be recognizable, but too far away to be
      reached by a cry or a gesture.
He is wearing a light-weight, brightly colored shirt.
His trousers belong to a suit, but the coat has been discarded.
His belt is narrow and somehow stays straightly on his pot belly.
His shoes are thin and shiny.
I think he bought those shoes on his last journey to Europe.
He is walking away, slowly.
He is wandering, meandering.
Sometimes he makes a little circle.
Sometimes he pauses and looks to one side or the other.
Sometimes he looks down.

Occasionally he looks up.

He never looks back, at least not directly.

Although he recedes very gradually and becomes very gradually
smaller, I continue to see all the aspects of his face and
figure clearly.

He is thinking about something and I know what.

It is not the place he now occupies in my life.

He cannot imagine that, only I can.

He is neither what he was (obviously), nor what he is (for I am
quite sure I am inventing that).

Is he Jim Wright? Is he not someone else?

Yes, he is Jim Wright. No, he is not someone else. (Who else could
he possibly be?)

When I die, he will arrive at where he is going. And I will set out
after him.

An Expatiation on the Combining of Weathers at Thirty-Seventh and Indiana Where the Southern More or Less Crosses the Dog

Oh, Ammons rolled the octaves slow
And the piano softened like butter in his hands,
And underward Catlett caught the beat
One sixteenth before the measure with a snip-snap touch on the
        snare
And a feathery brush on the cymbal, and Shapiro
Bowed the bass, half-glissing down past E-flat to A, to D,
And after a while
Berigan tested a limping figure low
In the cornet's baritone and raised it a third and then another
Until he was poised
On the always falling fulcrum of the blues,
And Bechet came in just as the phrase expired
And doubled it and inverted it
In a growl descending, the voice of the reed
Almost protesting, then to be made explicit
On the trombone as O'Brien took it
And raised it again, while Berigan stroked a high tone
Until it quavered and cried,
And Carruth achingly came on, the clarinet's most pure
High C-sharp, and he held it
Over the turn of the twelfth measure
And into the next verse with Bechet a fifth below rumbling
Upward on the back beat powerfully,

And O'Brien downward,
And Catlett press-rolling the slow beat now,
The old, old pattern of call and response unending,
And they felt the stir of the animal's soul in the cave,
And heard the animal's song,
Indefinable utterance, and saw
A hot flowing of the eternal, many-colored, essential plasm
As they leaned outward together, away from place, from time,
In one only person, which was the blues.

Sometimes When Lovers Lie Quietly Together, Unexpectedly One of Them Will Feel the Other's Pulse

'Tis just beyond mid-August. The summer has run mockingly
    away, as usual.
The first equinoctial storm has killed a certain paltry number of
    innocents in Galveston, who will be hardly missed,
And now its remnant brings a wind to Syracuse, a zephyrous wind
    that clears the air a little.
Not much. Haze lingers over the Bradford Hills.
What the Preacher said about retribution is true, true in the very
    nature of things, and therefore we Middle Americans must
    pay now
For our sins. I escaped, standing by the kitchen window, into my
    woodland soul
Where I saw our willow, the great eastern Maenad, Salix
    babylonica, toss her wild hair in sexual frenzy.
Then I went to my chair in the living room. I drank coffee and
    smoked, the relentless daily struggle to awaken.
Above the street at heavy opalescent noontime two electrical cables,
    strung from pole to pole,
Hung in relationship to one another such that the lower swung in
    and out of the shadow of the one above it,
And as it did so the sunlight reflected from it was sprung gleaming
    outward and inward along its length,
A steady expansion and contraction. And for a while I was taken
    away from my discontents
By this rhythm of the truth of the world, so fundamental, so
    simple, so clear.

The Necessary Impresario, Mr. Septic Tanck

Wally was so damn near right that his failure
Is a double sorrow. *Ach, wo ist die Mutter?*
For it was not a moral question with him, however
It ought to have been, and the god he lacked
Was the one that turns pumpkins into carriages.
For my part, "essence" is not quite the value
He hoped it was. Yet thanks to him the sunset
Fades. Did he know what he had done, there
In Hartford, of all places? We have reason
To believe he did, and also that he slept each
Moony night in his acceptance of his under-
Reaching, and muttered *"La maman, la maman"*
In his sleep. Unstatable, the idea of poetry,
Hence no idea—thinking, thinking, thinking.
The house was quiet and the night was irrelevant.
The poem is always something one slips under
Somebody's door. Then, anxiety. Or at last
Unremembrance, the fly wasted in winter's
Spiderweb in the corner of the porch. The park
We stroll in has no casino, or if it does, then
Only because the state arts council restored it.
The poem is a present for which we invent birthdays
Right and left. Or it is a leak in the cranium.
In thirty-two bars I can play anything and be
Happy.

The Impossible Indispensability of the *Ars Poetica*

But of course the poem is not an assertion. Do you see? When
    I wrote
That all my poems over the long years before I met you made you
    come true,
And that the poems for you since then have made you in yourself
    become more true,
I do not mean that the poems created or invented you. How many
    have foundered
In that sargasso! No, what I have been trying to say
For all the years of my awakening
Is that neither of the quaint immemorial views of poetry is
    adequate for us.
A poem is not an expression, nor is it an object. Yet it somewhat
    partakes of both. What a poem is
Is never to be known, for which I have learned to be grateful. But
    the aspect in which I see my own
Is as the act of love. The poem is a gift, a bestowal.
The poem is for us what instinct is for animals, a continuing and
    chiefly unthought corroboration of essence,
(Thought, however, ours and the animals', is useful).
Why otherwise is the earliest always the most important, the
    formative? The *Iliad*, the *Odyssey*, the *Book of Genesis*,
These were acts of love, I mean deeply felt gestures, which
    continuously bestow upon us
What we are. And if I do not know which poem of mine
Was my earliest gift to you,

Except that it had to have been written about someone else,
Nevertheless it was the gesture accruing value to you, your
        essence, while you were still a child, and thereafter
Across all these years. And see, see how much
Has come from that first sonnet after our loving began, the one
That was a kiss, a gift, a bestowal. This is the paradigm of
        fecundity. I think the poem is not
Transparent, as some have said, nor a looking-glass, as some have
        also said,
Yet it has almost the quality of disappearance
In its cage of visibility. It disperses among the words. It is a
        fluidity, a vapor, of love.
This, the instinctual, is what caused me to write "Do you see?"
        instead of "Don't you see?" in the first line
Of this poem, this loving treatise, which is what gives away the
        poem
And gives it all to you.

Of Distress Being Humiliated by the Classical Chinese Poets

Masters, the mock orange is blooming in Syracuse without scent,
     having been bred by patient horticulturists
To make this greater display at the expense of fragrance.
But I miss the jasmine of my back-country home.
Your language has no tenses, which is why your poems can never
     be translated whole into English;
Your minds are the minds of men who feel and imagine without
     time.
The serenity of the present, the repose of my eyes in the cool
     whiteness of sterile flowers.
Even now the headsman with his great curved blade and rank odor
     is stalking the byways for some of you.
When everything happens at once, no conflicts can occur.
Reality is an impasse. Tell me again
How the white heron rises from among the reeds and flies forever
     across the nacreous river at twilight
Toward the distant islands.

When I Wrote a Little

poem in the ancient mode for you
that was musical and had old words

in it such as would never do in
the academies you loved it and you

said you did not know how to thank
me and in truth this is a problem

for who can ever be grateful enough
for poetry but i said you thank me

every day and every night wordlessly
which you really do although again

in truth it is a problem for how can
life ever be consonant with spirit

yet we are human and are naturally
hungry for gratitude yes we need it

and never have enough oh my dear i
think these problems are always with

us and in reality have no solutions
except when we wash them away on

salty tides of loving as we rock in
the dark sure sea of our existence.

Survival as Tao, Beginning at 5:00 A.M.

Shadows in the room. Strange objects. The gladiolas Cindy bought,
      for instance,
The pink, deep red, yellow, and tangerine, these are all now more
      or less tropical and black,
somehow menacing in the huge earthenware pitcher, which
      resembles a sea anemone.
Three small mantas swim through. Insomnia, the *demonstratus* of
      the ground of despair,
Mixed with several kinds of tranquilizers: the mantas are not
      unexpected,
Nor is this atavistic sense of elsewhere. What is unexpected
Is this sentence by Leibnitz: "Music is an exercise in metaphysics
      while the mind does not know it is philosophizing."
I ought to look up the original, I do not care for
That word *exercise*, and I suspect an infelicitous translation.
L. himself was seldom infelicitous. But never mind the words for
      once, the statement catches at something
True and important. Music is the attempt to survive the unbearable
      through freedom from objectivity
Bestowed from outside, *i.e.*, by the variable frequencies of sound
      waves.
Loving Cindy, on the other hand, is an exercise, so-called, in
      metaphysics while the mind is perfectly aware,
For sex would be merely an objective conduct, an addiction,
      without the intellect to discover the meanings
Implicitly always in it. Loving Cindy is to survive the unbearable
      through freedom bestowed

From the inside, mutually. It is the only functional exercise in
	metaphysics still enduring, still
Enjoining our otherwise denatured sensibilities to perceive and
	understand the positive aspects of Being,
As the dawnlight indicates. The mantas swim away. The gladiolas,
	smiling lugubriously,
Deposit the unbearable upon the day, that is, their lower blossoms,
	withered overnight.
Coffee and cigarettes in my Chinese bath robe. The day, Sunday,
	will be hotter than yesterday, Saturday, which was
Hotter than the day before, Friday, etc. Now Kate's television emits
	the most incredible
Noises I have ever heard. Where's the music? (*"Wo ist die musik?"*
	the Bo said, so many years ago.) No one
Remembers how it was made, except I—*ego, scriptor.*
Yet in the freedom of orgasm my thoughts of her
Are indeed a song, a metaphysical song, a soaring in the
	inconceivable, brought to the fullness of harmony
By her thoughts of me.

Ovid, Old Buddy, I Would Discourse
with You a While

upon mutability—if it were possible. But you don't
know me. Already you cannot conceive my making the second line
of a poem so much longer than the first.
No matter, mutability is the topic, and I see you there exiled on the
   Thracian shore
among those hairy mariners speaking an improbable tongue,
a location of you damnably similar to Syracuse, N.Y., and I see
you addressing your first letter to the new emperor, Tiberius,
looking blankly out to the rocks and the gray ocean
as you search for rhythms and awesome words to make this
the greatest verse-epistle ever written and obtain your pardon, your
   freedom to return
to Rome, so long denied by Augustus.
Do you know me, after all? But of course, how could you not when
   my words are your very bones?
You speak to me of two thousand years of solitude.
Yes, you are writing that letter forever.
You tell me how you cannot name your crime because you only
   suspect what it is
and to name it would make it true.
You are innocent. Tiberius will not grant you pardon. He cannot.
But he can fling those victims, stopped forever wild-eyed in mid-air,
   off the precipice at Capreae!
Some powers are always powerless.
The change from Augustus to Tiberius, what does it mean,

that instant of mutability continuing forever
between a death and an investiture?
You whisper to me, No pardon, no pardon, no pardon,
and the three sprigs of white lilac in the glass pitcher on my table
that are slightly, but only slightly, wilted—
the stems weakened, the heavy blossom-clusters depending—
tremble as if a wind even from Olympus were meandering through
       the room.

The Sociology of Toyotas and Jade Chrysanthemums

Listen here, sistren and brethren, I am goddamn tired
of hearing you tell me how them poor folk, especially
black, have always got a Cadillac parked in the front
yard, along with the flux of faded plastic and tin.
I just blew fourteen thou, which make no mistake is
the bankroll, on a Toyota Celica. "The poor man's
sports car," the salesman said, which is the truth.
(I'll write about the wrongs done to car salesmen
another time.) She do look mighty good there in my
front yard, too, all shiny red and sleek as a seal.
It means a lot to me, like something near or almost
near what I've always wanted, and it reminds me of
the Emperor Tlu whose twenty-first wife asked him what
he wanted for his birthday, and he being a modest man
said the simplest thing he could think of off-hand,
a jade chrysanthemum, and thirty years later he got it,
because you see that's how long it took the master
jade-carver and his apprentices to make it, and when
he got it—Tlu, that is—he keeled over on the instant
in sheer possessive bliss. Why not? Professor Dilthey
once said history is the science of inexactly recording
human inexact passions, thereby giving birth to sociologists,
as every schoolperson knows. Well, let them have a look
at all these four-wheeled jade chrysanthemums around here.

Working

My dear, what we know most,
You and I, is the unrelenting
Awareness of being our own future
In the mode of not-being. Perhaps I
Know it better than you, or differently,
I so much closer to death than you are.
Or perhaps not-being is a mode of the absolute
And it comes to the same thing.
I watch you. Of course I have many friends
Who are writers and who offer me
Their putatively finished poems
From time to time, and students—
La, St. Harmonie, more than enough!
But never have I lived before
With a writer, never have seen
The inception, the failure, the mending
In anyone's poems but my own. To see
You at work, to watch you, to observe
The relentlessness of becoming
Stopped, held in your voice—
Yours, yes, lisping a little there on the page—
This is joy, pain, indignation, fear, exuberance, so much
And so mixed that I end
In wonderment only.
It is a *wonder*. It is *wonderful*.
That strange Akademiker (but finally agreeable),

Herr Doktor Martin Heidegger, wrote:
". . . in the phenomenon of willing
The underlying totality of care shows through,"
And he meant *willing* and *care* in all their
Philological weight, as I do too.
This is the wonder. This is what I see now.
I see it here in our home, here
Where you work, here
Where we both work,
Separate and always
Together.

"The World as Will and Representation"

When I consider the children of the middle class
as representations of phenomena to my subject sense
I can hardly see them at all, they fade
into the shrubbery, of which a superabundance
is *sui generis* their world. I am likely to be overwhelmed,
or distracted, leaning my mind on some green bosom.
But then they are things-in-themselves, these children,
and their glee is a thing-in-itself, their exuberance
as they terrorize one another, wiping themselves out
in a continuum of destruction, themselves
as surrogates of parents. But the parents remain
representations, never things-in-themselves, but only
shadow-figures taking out the garbage; and thus
the Will of Schopenhauer's essay leaps out at me
in children-in-themselves, starker than stones or stars,
so that I cower; for the future is theirs, day by day
they remove it from the plastic wrap of not-being
and leave it on the death-strewn lawns. Yes, if will
is all we know of ourselves as things, and thence
of all things, how can I not infer a radical divergence
of degree between everything else and children? The spirea
dies, the little nebulae of viburnum wink out in willing
whatness, but the children's shrieks of bliss and triumph
are merciless, raging from another world, another time,
in causalities I cannot properly discern or identify,
so that all understanding is blocked and thrust back
as mere knowledge, odious data, nauseating demonstrations,
these relentless present children of the middle class.

To Know in Reverie the Only Phenomenology
of the Absolute

Why was it Bavaria? The house in the forest
was modest, a cabin, though rather substantial
with latticework on the porch, a window in the gable.
Each afternoon I walked to the village
down a woodland path among great dark trees,
across a bridge made of cedar poles. Patches
of violets and forget-me-nots. At the café
I smoked a cigar, drank coffee or lemonade,
read a newspaper, wrote postcards, an occasional
letter. I talked with the proprietor.
I walked home at twilight and rested
on the bridge, looking down into the stream,
the weeds oscillating in clear water. I carried a stout
walkingstick, a staff really, cut from a straight
ash sapling. I did this for years in my
old age, and in the gable room wrote a number
of better-than-average books. But I have never been
in Bavaria.

Meditation in the Presence of "Ostrich Walk"

Of the two cardinals the female is both bolder and more "beautiful."
    She comes
To the railing, crest raised high, snapping her eyes this way and
    that,
Uttering the little nasal ech-ech of fear and belligerence,
Then down to the lower travis, then finally to the flagstones, where
    she feeds.
Now comes the male, seeing the way is safe, and begins to hull
    seeds and feed them
To her. The mind performs its wearisome gyrationing. The female
    accepts
These token mouthfuls, but eats on her own between them. She is
    very obviously
Able to take care of herself. Although most people say otherwise,
    and say so vehemently,
The difference between Floyd Bean and Joe Sullivan is distinct,
    crucial,
And unique. I move my hand to rewind the tape and the cardinals
Are gone forever. *Ora pro nobis,* my good St. Chance, my darling.

No Supervening Thought of Grace

for Galway

My true friend's poems about aging and death held my mind as in
      a sea-surge
this afternoon, for they are true poems, and good ones,
and I myself feel weakened much of the time now from the nights
      of death-laden insomnia,
which no weakness cures.
Almost equinox. A cold March day in Saratoga with hesitating rain
      in the pines.
Beyond the woods, rushing cars and trucks on the interstate
make a continual sound of rising and falling, a seething almost like
      the sea,
which is almost like the sound of my friend's poems.
But he is five or six years younger than I, what does he know?
And what does anyone know? Here, here is where it is, here in my
      own skull.
Well, soon enough he will learn. And so will everyone.
I went out walking in the woods with my hands in my pockets,
thinking and brooding, because like the sea trees are important,
      and rain is important,
and the important wet brown needles were springy beneath my
      feet
that nevertheless went falteringly, cautious for the litter of wet
      downed limbs,
the boneyard of the pines.

I found a half-buried old wax-paper Dixie cup
almost like a fungus, stained softly gray in a flocky pattern edged
        with coral and orange. Sometimes one doesn't care
any longer about oneself, but for a true, five-or-six-year-younger
        friend
one would dash into the sea, if that would help,
one would beseech the gods.

No Matter What, After All, and That Beautiful Word So

This was the time of their heaviest migration,
And the wild geese for hours sounded their song
In the night over Syracuse, near and far,
As they circled toward Beaver Lake up beyond
Baldwinsville. We heard them while we lay in bed
Making love and talking, and often we lay still
Just to listen. "What is it about that sound?"
You said, and because I was in my customary
Umbrage with reality I answered, "Everything
Uncivilized," but knew right away I was wrong.
I examined my mind. In spite of our loving
I felt the pressure of the house enclosing me,
And the pressure of the neighboring houses
That seemed to move against me in the darkness,
And the pressure of the whole city, and then
The whole continent, which I saw
As the wild geese must see it, a system
Of colored lights creeping everywhere in the night.
Yes, the McDonald's on the strip outside Casper,
Wyoming (which I could indistinctly remember),
Was pressing against me. "Why permit it?"
I asked myself. "It's a dreadful civilization,
Of course, but the pressure is yours." It was true.
I listened to the sound in the sky, and I had no
Argument against myself. The sound was unlike
Any other, indefinable, unnameable—certainly

Not a song, as I had called it. A kind of discourse,
The ornithologists say, in a language unknown
To us; a complex discourse about something
Altogether mysterious. Yet so is the cricketing
Of the crickets in the grass, and it is not the same.
In the caves of Lascaux, I've heard, the Aurignacian
Men and women took leave of the other animals, a trauma
They tried to lessen by painting the animal spirits
Upon the stone. And the geese are above our window.
Oh, what is it about that sound? Talking in the sky,
Bell-like words, but only remotely bell-like,
A language of many and strange tones above us
In the night at the change of seasons, talking unseen,
An expressiveness—is that it? Expressiveness
Intact and with no meaning? Yet we respond,
Our minds make an answering, though we cannot
Articulate it. How great the unintelligible
Meaning! Our lost souls flying over. The talk
Of the wild geese in the sky. It is there. It is so.

"Sure," Said Benny Goodman,

"We rode out the depression on technique." How gratifying and
      how rare,
Such expressions of a proper modesty. Notice it was not said
By T. Dorsey, who could not play a respectable "Aunt Hagar's" on
      a kazoo,
But by the man who turned the first jazz concert at Carnegie Hall
Into an artistic event and put black musicians on the stand with
      white ones equally,
The man who called himself Barefoot Jackson, or some such,
In order to be a sideman with Mel Powell on a small label
And made good music on "Blue Skies," etc. He knew exactly who
      he was, no more, no less.
It was rare and gratifying, as I've said. Do you remember the Incan
      priestling, Xtlgg, who said,
"O Lord Sun, we are probably not good enough to exalt thee," and
      got himself
Flung over the wall at Machu Picchu for his candor?
I honor him for that, but I like him because his statement implies
That if he had foreseen the outcome he might not have said it.
But he did say it. *Candor seeks its own unforeseeable occasions.*
Once in America in a dark time the existentialist flatfoot floogie
      stomped across the land
Accompanied by a small floy floy. I think we shall not see their
      like in our people's art again.

Language As Inevitable Metaphor. Idea As Inevitable Figment

. . . for we all of us, grave or light, get our thoughts entangled
in metaphors, and act fatally on the strength of them.

—George Eliot

I mind once on a forenoon in early summer sitting
On his side-steps with old Steve Washer that was, reading
The paper and talking about the craziness of that year's
Election campaigns, the way people do, though it was long ago
When I was a young fellow about 45, and I don't remember
Who were the elephants and the jackasses, or which we most
     disfavored,
Or whether we gave it much of a nevermind, but after a while
The topic wore out, don't you know, and we sat silent together
Looking out toward the barn or across the road to the orchard
And the day pasture which were a smitch hazy in the warm sun,
And then I said, sort of half afraid—because that was
Vermont, of course, and folk there don't concert overmuch
With sentiment, though happen once in a swath of days they do,
And then it's twice as commodious, if you see my meaning—
I said, "Mr. Washer, you have a mighty good-looking farm," to
     which
He made no answer for a time, squinting out at the ancient ellum
That rose and descended again on the knob of the pasture,
And then he said, "I guess. I guess you might say for now
It's in a pretty good state of cultivation."

                                        I guess I might have.
Tidy it was, with all those smooth green knolls and swales
And the trees and all, but I recollect the colors most, I think,
All spring and summer, dandelions and bluets, mustard and vetch,
The buttercups that cows won't eat, and daisies and hawkweed
And black-eyed susans and joe pye weed and goldenrod, so many
Wonderful weeds, the meadow rue and salsifee—I don't rightly
Conceive how many any more—the weeds, we called them, though
We meant something a shade different in the word and we let
Them grow, thistle and yarrow and all. Not like here.
Look, the little lawns, the hedges, those foreign-appearing
Trees, but the lawns mostly, squared off and snubbed tight, grass
So bright it looks prefabricated, pre-*cultivated*, or like green
Plastic it might be, with nary weeds. Why, they even do off
The violets. I believe there's a thing like over-tidiness, or call it
Over-cultivation, that's more the nub, old proven ways grown
Lopsidal and disproportionate, cultivation for no purpose
And too refined, and the weeds poisoned. Who could have reckoned
People would put poison on the land? Of course I'm nothing,
An old man stopping here a spell before he goes his journey.
Like as not I'm misremembering. But it seems as though
I most could see those colors still and smell the sweetness
On the air at sunset, when the swallows glean the sky.

A Post-Impressionist Susurration for the
First of November, 1983

Does anything get more tangled and higgeldy-piggeldy than the
      days as they drop all jumbled and
One by one on the historical heap? Not likely. And so we are all, in
      spite of ourselves, jackstraw diarists.
This afternoon we went walking on the towpath of the Erie Canal,
      which was strangely
Straight and narrow for our devious New England feet. Yet it was
      beautiful, a long earthen avenue
Reaching far ahead of us into the shifting gossamer veils that hung
      everywhere in folds, oaks clinging to their dark leaves,
Bare maples in their many shades of gray, the field of goldenrod
      gone to seed and burnt-out asters,
Sumac with dark cones, the brown grasses, and at the far edge,
      away from the canal,
A line of trees above which towered three white pines in their
      singular shapes.
I have never seen a white pine growing naturally that was not
      unique and sculpturesque.
Why should one not devote one's life to photographing white
      pines, as Bentley of Jericho
Spent his photographing snowflakes? But it's too late, of course.
      At all events the colors,
Not forgetting cattails and milkweed, dock and sorbaria, ferns and
      willows and barberries,
Were a nearly infinite variety of the soft tones, the subtle tones,
      made even more indistinct

In their reflections on the greenish water of the canal. And a light
    breeze was blowing.
For once I will risk the word *zephyr*, which is right and which
    reminds me of *sapphire*,
And I realize that beneath all these colors lay an undertone of blue,
    the gentle sky as it curls
Below the penumbra of vision. A small yellow butterfly tricked its
    way across the brown field beside us,
And I thought to myself, Where in hell did you come from? Last
    night was a hard frost.
And then I knew it had been born this day, perhaps a moment ago,
    and its life was flickering, flickering out in our presence
As we walked with our hands in a lovers' clasp on the straight
    towpath beside the canal that made us think
Of France, of tumbling autumn days, of hundreds and hundreds
    and hundreds of loves and visions.
Sometimes Cindy is half ill, sometimes more than half, because she
    doesn't know as much
As people she envies. She writes poems about not knowing, about
    the anguish over knowledge,
And when I was her age I felt the same way. I know that anguish.
    I used to be pained especially
Because I could not name the colors I saw, and I envied painters
    their knowledge of pigments,
I studied the charts of colors and I looked up the names—mallow,
    cerise—in the dictionary,
I examined the meanings of *hue, shade, tone, tint, density,
    saturation, brilliance,* and so on,
But it did no good. The eye has knowledge the mind cannot share,
    which is why painters

So often are inarticulate. Is the eye ignorant, uneducated? How
　　　absurd. That would be impossible.
Hence I became eventually, gradually, unashamed of my mind's
　　　incapacity, just as I had once written
Poems to be read many times, but what was the use of that? Now
　　　I write poems to be read once and forgotten,
Or not to be read at all.

"I've Never Seen Such a Real Hard Time Before":
Three-Part Invention

Having planted our little Northern Spy at the wrong season,
Having pruned it in trepidation and ignorance, having watched it
Do nothing at all for a month in the drought-burned, weedy
        wasteland
Of the front yard—that prefiguring desolation!—now I am
Uplifted truly
By the sapling's big new leaves and its stems lengthening,
And my mind carries everywhere I go this image of a fresh, pale,
        green upsprouting
In the form of a fountain, a small, natural, simple fountain;

And having learned at last, from an intelligent and willing young
        man
Behind the counter at Superior Sound, Inc., on East Erie Boulevard,
The definitive and conclusive difference between a ceramic and a
        magnetic
Cartridge for my stereo turntable,
Having placed this sparkle of knowledge in my mind like a jewel
        on a dark velvet ground,
I glance at it hundreds of times in passing, so to speak,
With a little thrill of gratification for its novelty, its actuality,
And especially for its purity, its unfailing, useless betokening of
        what is:

And every day these twinges of pain in my heart, that muscle
        unenvisionable,

Draining me downward like the "flow of atoms" into cool organic
      earth,
The quicksand,
Downward in this strange new fluidity, this impersonal dissolution,
Drawn by an energy somehow inside me and yet not mine—
How stunning the methodical magnitudes of force!—
Make me wonder, somewhat abstractedly, about the pulverization
      of the soul,
About vast windy wastes of crumbled joys and drifting knowledge,
      about what becomes
Of all the disjuncted dregs of consciousness:

This song is a wave forever rolling among
      the stars.

Letter to Maxine Sullivan

Just when I imagined I had conquered
nostalgia so odious, had conquered Vermont and the half-dozen
        good years there,
here you come singing "A Cottage for Sale," which is a better than
        average song as a matter of fact, though that's
not saying much and it's been lost to my memory for years and
        years,
but you always had good taste, meaning the same as mine.
Oh Maxine, how screwed up everything is.
Your voice in 1983 is not altogether what it was in 1943,
nor are the Swedish All Stars up to the standard of John Kirby,
        Russ Procope, Buster Bailey, Charlie Shavers, Billy Kyle,
        and—but who was on drums? Ben Thigpen? Shadow
        Wilson?—
the names, names, lovely old names calling to me always through
        echoing dark; no, nostalgia will never be conquered—
yet your singing is as passionate as ever, evinced in these exact
        little accents and slurs and hesitations, the marvelous
        stop-time measures, the *languets* of song,
so that I am overcome by your musical excellence and also by
        anger and sorrow because everyone
hoo-hahs so outrageously over Ella Fitzgerald, the eternal
        bobby-soxer (and millionaire).
You, a black woman singing a white Tin Pan Alley tune in Sweden
        about my home back in Vermont,
and I in Syracuse, where the jasmine has no scent—

feelings and values scattering as the death-colored leaves scatter on
        this windy day.
Maxine, I cling to you, I am your spectral lover, both of us
        crumbling now, but our soul-dust mingling nevertheless
in the endless communion of song, and I hope, I believe, that you
        have striven, as I have,
beyond the brute moments of nostalgia,
into the timelessness of music,
and that you have someone with you, as I have Cindy.

The Circumstances of Meditation This Morning
Led Me to the Cigar of Johannes Brahms

But the circumstances
are always and always
different and the same,
being simply my
life. And the joy
I saw there in him as
he was in my life
this morning, and I
knew his mind, how it
played with those
ingenuities of Chopin's
ballades that had
seemed difficult beyond
understanding once, but
now stolen and assimilated
and forgotten—no, no,
not forgotten, the quiet
little gratification of
conquest never set
aside, yet in his mind
the sweet somberness
of contralto, viola,
and the mid-range of
piano, most definitely
not epiphanic, but a

melting and mingling and
an interfusion that
is familiar precisely
in its never having been
heard before, oh, the
joy, beyond ego, be-
yond the fracturing
stones of the objective
world, the strata, the
massive tablets of
God—bah! that simple-
minded Eckhart, what
did he know, being not
a musician, not out
here in the garden of
sensational thought?
The smoke of the cigar
rolls and twines with
just this supple
sensuosity of the
voices. (Did Der
Herr Meister ever have
a cigar?) Never, Brahms
said, trust a man who
does not know the qualities
of good tobacco,
and so I say, so say
I! Walking in his
roundish body with hands

clasped behind, among
the vaporing
roses of his mind's
song, he feels
the blood coursing
and the tingle and
stir of his penis, that
most intimate, secret
corroboration, and he
does not need to smile,
it is beyond smiling,
it is a continuum of
experience in the place
of the self-swelling-
within. Begone, you
dreams!—take philo-
sophy with you. I
compose, therefore I
am not. And today,
this morning? Out
there? Yes, the Lebanese
dyings, not like
Lionel Barrymore so
many times in his cosy
deathbed, but like the
red-tailed hawk on
Interstate 90 that
stooped on a ground
hog and became con-

fused in the speeding
traffic and was hit
by the upper front of
a trailer tractor
rig, was hit and ex-
ploded, feathers and
blood, oh, my god, the
horror in my eyes,
how insane can this
world be, for the child
was ripped inside
out this morning, the
pregnant girl was
blown backward fifty
feet into the toppling
wall, all at
once, the fat contempt-
ible moment. Only
then the necessity of
these deaths, their
utter awful unavailing
indispensability, for
what is not needed is
the cigar in the bland
head at the end of
the conference table,
smoke trailing into
the soundless air-
conditioner hidden

somewhere behind the
hidden lights. Let
an end be made of
tables and chairs! Man
on his feet is not
conspiratorial. So
begone, you who would
call me your countryman,
I am none of yours, I
am capable of dis-
tinctions, I am the
cigar of Johannes
Brahms. May you be
no deaths but only
a vanishment. Let
emptiness be where you
are tomorrow morning.
I cry out these lines
without sound. I cry
them out. Listen.

By Finitude in Its Several Manifestations
Freedom Is Qualified

The wind in the chimney makes a song, finitude, finitude, while we
       cherish our freedom from the storm, as people
always have, believing, no doubt naturally, that freedom is from
       the world and found in the technology of building;
and as some people, many people, believe now that freedom from
       the inevitability of worldly human evil
is found in the technology of explosive grains of reality. But is not
       the technology of the brickmakers and bricklayers
what captures for us the song of the wind? Has not this always
       been true for those who know the rudiments of song?

On the Truistical and Fashionable Eyes of Albert Camus

Both Cicero and Ruskin noted that behind their intelligence is a
    muted quality.
For which we have no name.
Takagawa too.
Only an inhuman society engenders it, and this is well known,
But rarely does it enter the divagations of policy.
Nevertheless after a century and a half
Schopenhauer, that good man, perceptibly begins to prevail over
    the *Phänomenologie des Geistes*, that horror.
All art aspires to the condition of music. Repeat, aspires.

Une Présence Absolue

Not aware of it much of the time, but of course we are
Heedless folk, under the distracting stars, among the great cedars,
And so we give to ourselves casual pardon. It is there, though,
     always,
The continuum of what really is, what only is.
The rest is babble and furiosity. Imagination, let me pay more
     attention to you,
You alone have this letting power; give me your one gift, which is
     the one absolution.
I am this poor stupid bastard half-asleep here under this bridge.

Poem Catching Up with an Idea

Freedom is not to be proved but is rather a postulate
of action. Thus excellent Berdyaev,
who has meant much to me,
although I must shake my head and make a face
when he undertakes to explain
the Holy Ghost. We are unbelievers,
which may be (I regularly
think it is) our misfortune. But we are still
existentialist lovers.
Strange Søren Kierkegaard of Hamlet's province
would approve of us in our unchurchly dark
devotions. In Syracuse the rain falls every day,
the faces of the burghers of Edgehill Road
are as bland as marshmallows and as puffy.
To live here, to love here,
as Jack our friend the Gilbert would say,
sighing, smiling,
requires an extraordinary knowledge of freedom,
unhistorical and reinvented by us here in every
act, as when I brought to you for a love token
the plastic sack of just sprouted lilies-of-the-valley
to plant around the steps of our arched doorway.
That was phenomenon, not poetry, not symbol, the act
without a proof, freedom-in-love.

How Lewisburg, Pa., Escaped the Avenging Angel

"Dust," she said. "What is it? Where does it come from?"

"What do you mean dust?" I said.

"Dust," she said. "That stuff that comes back on top of the
    refrigerator three days after you've wiped it off."

"Lint," I said. "Bits of soil. Danders. Carbon. Vegetable matter."

"Oh," she said.

"Generalized metaphysical fall-out," I said. "Dust to dust, etc."

"How do you know?" she said.

"I don't," I said.

"Then kindly refrain from being so fucking authoritative," she said.

Underground the Darkness Is the Light

When I first started out to make what later became known as
    Hayden's Runaway Pond, I borrowed
Baldy Langdell's little Cat that he used mostly for sap-gathering
    in his hillside sugar orchard
Over in Waterville, but he had a blade on it, and once I got the
    hose connections tight
It worked well. I had a good spot, and Pop Foster, the county
    agricultural agent,
Agreed. "Ideal," he said. It was a gentle downslope sort of folded
    in the middle, where a brook
Ran straight down from a spring in the woods behind, a good
    spring, never known
To run less than nine quarts a minute in the driest season. I went to
    work.
"Now watch you don't scrape too deep in the hardpan," Pop said,
    and I nodded.
I pushed dirt to all sides, but mostly to the front, where the
    embankment would be highest,
Like a dam. Pop showed me how to set up the standpipe with a
    wing valve at the bottom, the outlet pipe
Headed straight forward under the bank and into the brookbed
    again. It didn't take long,
A day and a half with the dozer. Then I set the valve just a mite
    open
So some of the water would continue flowing out into the brook
    and on downstream,

But enough would catch in the pond to fill it. I watched. Slow, very
     slow, only a puddle
After the first two days. But I expected that. I sowed the banks to
     rye, clover, and orchard grass.
Of course that summer, after the pond filled and water spilled into
     the standpipe so I could close the bottom valve,
It was a sterile pond. But the next spring I had frogs, big ones and
     little ones, and that summer
What I call the purple water flower seeded in and some bulrushes
     on the far side. Then the following spring
The stoneflies hatched, and the mosquitoes, so I stocked some
     minnows and brim. By end of July
I had a muskrat hole on the upper back just over the water-line.
     Next spring I stocked brookies,
A couple of dozen, and they took to it, and I used to go at twilight
     with my part-shepherd bitch Locky
To feed those trout bits of hamburger. How they rose to it! Locky
     would stand downbank
With her front paws extended and bark at them, and sometimes I
     thought maybe the trout
Were barking back. It was a fine pond, alive, a going concern.
     Swallows from Marshall's barn
Skimming the surface. Once I saw a heron. Then two summers later
     I saw the water
Was sinking. "Must have scratched the bottom a mite hard," Pop
     said. It went down slowly
The same way it had filled, but after six weeks it was all gone,
     nothing left
But mud and the brook trickling across the bottom and down into
     a hole I could see plain enough,

Jagged, about eight inches across. No fish, no frogs. They must
    have gone down too.
Down into the earth, a live pond flowing into all those channels and
    chambers down there.
Strange to think of. Locky went trotting and sniffing here and there
    on the sun-dried mud,
Looking half scared. "Don't that beat all?" Marshall said. And I
    said, "Yes, it does."

Cross My Heart and Hope to Die,
It Was the Very Same Song Exactly

Where does the sadness come from? The great Seychellesan tortoise
      that heaved its quarter-ton of body up onto legs
Plainly misengineered to support it and tottered a few yards
      uncertainly across the grass and gravel
Seemed old enough to know, so wrinkled and outcast. Out of the
      air then? Some distillation of the color green?
This was at Clyde Peeling's Reptileland south of Williamsport on
      Rte. 15 in Pennsylvania,
Which is not a mere tourist trap. Mr. Peeling knows his animals
      and studies them. He treats them well.
But on the subject of sadness he only turned his gaze eastward,
      like the tortoise, toward the Muncy Hills.
The eyes of the tortoise are as beautiful as any I've ever seen,
      perfectly almond-shaped, brown and deeply lustrous,
And they are filmed with tears. My companion was on the verge
      of tears herself, I knew this in the same way that she
Knew the animal's sorrow. If women ruled the world—real women,
      not the blurry rag dolls cast up by the sea of history
Like any detritus—it would be a sadder, saner place. Old age
      accedes, which is not wisdom precisely but the best we
      can do.
(Yet where does the sadness come from, this saturation of
      everything, this seepage into the world?)
Women are the true pragmatists, and William James is their best
      friend, if they only knew it. They are also sentimentalists,
      which is not

The paradox it may seem, for what should the end of the universe,
   this "heap," elicit if not love? The end is what
Women have been talking about since before the last ice age. Hence
   they are passionate as well as pragmatic.
Balzac wrote: "All passions are essentially Jesuitical," and indeed
   this is almost a truth—as close as we are likely to get
In our promiscuous knowing called language—but is passion
   therefore somehow inferior? It sees all things
And insists on distinctions, and it never gives up, but this does not
   mean fury, it does not necessarily mean pride.
Are not we, in what is left of our own vestigial and unselfconscious
   instinct, seeking the cognitive mode of the animals
And of women, we with our programmed thinking machines? The
   sadness is the mystery of beginning, a parchment map with
   terra incognita
Inscribed on the northeastern sector. The sun shone brilliantly over
   Pennsylvania in late May.
Now it is August and hazy, and we are elsewhere, remembering
   that the tortoise with its tearful eyes was not looking at us.

II

MOTHER

Margery Carruth, 1896–1981

"O thou great Nothing, thou Indifference, thou Forgetfulness, has not She in her own nature the right to be meaningless? To be what in their nature words cannot contain, the less than meaningless?"
—*Sadhu Jinri-Ghoramnya*

1.   The Event

Mother, now at last I must speak to you. The hour, so late but even
      so, has come.
Mother, after sixty-one and a half years of my life,
After one and one-quarter years of your death,
After your incomprehensible durance and anguish, which deranges
      me still,
After the wordless years between us, our unutterable, constricted,
      strangling chaos,
After the long years of my private wrecked language, when my
      mind shook in the tempests of fear,
After everything between us is done and never to be undone, so
      that no speech matters,
Nevertheless I must speak.

The sea is not here, nor has it ever in my life been where I was,
Nor was it more than briefly ever in yours (you, bound inland,
      away from your desire),
Yet how you spoke, sixty percent aphasic as you were,
Of "the water" and "the ship," and of "the glittering water" or
      "the golden shining water"
Between the ship and the pier when you looked down from the
      fantail,
(Was she the *Vulcania*? I almost seem to remember),
How you spoke in the phantasmic childhood you were living again
Of the water gleaming, of your mother, of her leaping down into
      that golden alley of death,

(But she did not; she leapt from the sixteenth floor of a hotel on
      Broadway),

How your pallid, brown-spotted, wrinkled, half-paralyzed
      countenance grimaced,

So that I could not tell whether you were smiling or struck with
      terror,

Until I recognized that it was the ultimate human expression, the
      two masks superimposed,

Mother, how you spoke then, giggling and whimpering, your voice
      skipping from node to node of your mind's dispersion,

How you mingled the water, the glimmering, the exhilaration of a
      voyage beginning, the horror of a voyage ending,

(Your mother, my Nana, the strange woman of glistening auburn
      hair),

How you spoke gave me to understand the as it seemed inhuman
      human lucency

Of your half-dead mind,

And the way, intermingling there, these visions of childhood,
      death, mother, and water

Were the wisdom beyond speech,

Were knowledge in its clearest configuration,

Which did not for one minutest part of an instant relieve your
      agony.

"O Hayden, take me home," you wailed, singing it out fully and
      tremulously.

But you thought home was England.

Was your damaged brain the same as a damaged soul?

I ask myself, and have asked in long, long sequences of
      perturbation and doubt,

(I who have called and called to my own soul and never heard an
		answer),
You lay there three years, twisted,
Until your body became so rigid that no man could have been
		strong enough
To undo the knot, as no person, man or woman or even child,
Could penetrate your mind in its writhing, its convulsive
		indagation.
Oh, the suffering! You in the focus of the pain of all our lives,
You there on the threshold, knowing it clearly, peering into the
		darkness,
But so ravaged in the coils of thought that no current could be
		induced,
And thus you lay there smashed, a machine of random parts, of no
		definable function,
Unable to generate so much as the least beginning spark of an idea,
Unable to conceive any *suppositum* of your predicament,
And fear wailed out of you, unintelligible sentences that vanished
		in rising tremolo,
As if you were an animal somehow granted the power to know
		but not to think,
Or as if you were a philosopher suddenly deprived of every faculty
		except
Original fear and pathos. I cannot surmise a state of being more
		inconsonant
With human consciousness.
Oh, many as evil, many and many, God knows, but none
		essentially worse.

To which was added, of course, humiliation.

"I am not nice," you repeated in your weeping quaver. "I am not
    nice,"
Covered from head to foot with your own shit.

Once when I came you would not acknowledge me. Not even a
        flicker of your eyelid.
I thought you were dead.
I shook you as it seemed unmercifully and shouted next to your
        ear. I shouted.
At last, unmoving, you said in a quiet, perfectly normal voice, as
        in old times,
"I hear you."
Nothing more. After an hour I left.
Never have I heard anything more terrible than that "I hear you."

Three years. For you they could have been three million. You lived
        only
In the present moment,
The moment before death.
And the doctors who had "saved your life" would give you
        nothing.
Three million moments before death.
Should I have smuggled in marijuana for you? Heroin? I think I
        should.
A century ago the doctors would have fed you laudanum like sugar
        cubes,
Assuming you had lived through your first stroke. But you would
        not have.
You would have died quickly, appropriately, humanly.

For every technical advance, intelligence makes a moral regression.

Three million moments. Three million deaths. O my mother.
You lying there in a twisted, useless body.
You on the shore of death, perpetually.
You in the shadowy tumult of memories.
You with your language broken, stammering, whole aggregates of
    once-luminous words blown out.
You nearly blind, your son's face unrecognizable.
You with your hearing still acute, able to distinguish voices.
You with your radio that the nurses always tuned to a rock station,
    in spite of your frowning.
You unable to cover yourself, your withered cunt showing.
You wailing and wailing, no, not like a child, but in a voice torn
    and wasted, a cruel parody of a child.
You with your teeth broken and rotted like the barely discernible,
    almost effaced lines of an ancient wooden sculpture (and the
    doctors would permit no dentistry for fear the shock would
    "kill" you).
You there, always and forever there, in the termination that
    obliterates everything else.
O my mother.

2. The Water

I think I know why in death's unrelenting moment you thought of
      the water, the ship, and your mother,
And of your mother's death,
("I think," so common, so perilous a verbal alibi),
For this is the technology of intellection in our time, state-of-the-art,
How are implanted in every childhood the great emblems of our
      being, one way or another,
Then to roil fomenting like magma in our deepest centers,
      managing us whether we will or no,
For did not the land rise from the sea? Oh, consider that spasm:
Did not you erupt from the amniotic fluid of your mother's uterus,
      as I from yours?
That sea whose currents, swaying, are the flow of motherhood
      through all our idea of time,
From the earliest parturition,
From the first warming of blood,
From the primeval rising and falling, the moist vapors and
      condensations,
The warmth of the remote sun nevertheless occurring here on this
      stony shore, this wall, this hospital,
And our returning through all existence to the tidal source, death
      in the water and forgetting.

Once I sat on a bluff by the Susquehanna, that broad green fluvium,
I looked backward beyond the near diagonal slope to the broad
      field undulating,

A farmer ploughing there, guiding the share in the furrows behind
his horse in the old way,
Patiently, steadily, a man familiar with the good way of loving,
And the field was writhing in her corresponsiveness,
But as if all the declensions of intelligence with its smeared graphia
had blurred my vision,
I could not see if she moved in pleasure or pain,
O rainlike sun, O earthen sea.

How was it when you were ploughed?
Not aphasia can be the cause why you never said
In all the clinging cries of your long death
The word for your husband.

O my mother, how we have in paltry intelligence made a foul
language,
For do not we say "conceiving"
To mean both the transactions of love in nature and the
negotiations of thought in emptiness?

The land risen, streaming in all her vulval channels, the fecund
mud,
The loam ploughed and harrowed (oh language of violence) and
dark and clean,
The corn sprouting, green leaflets, rows curving with the contours
of earth's body,
The worms working the soil and the swaggering crow lording and
eating,

Could you in the chaos of misery, the wound of your ancient sex
       aroused and stinging under death's touch,
Make any conceiving of these conflicting emblems?
Or shall I say that before intelligence, pleasure and pain simply
       were, and were one,
The undifferentiated sensing, without discrimination?
No. But for you were we all hagseed.
But for you.

When an old woman, staring blind, her skeleton, the skull and
       bones, showing almost white
Beneath the mantle of her dissolving skin,
Dies at last,
We rejoice and say that she is a bride again, and we give her
       flowers,
Virgin of the sea, girl of the sun,
—And mother, I could bide no more in these damnable
Inconsistencies, fear-wrought, flimsy, hysterical,
And I saw we are right to rejoice, a small, reluctant celebration of
       the drowned mind,
For the passage out of consciousness is at least in itself a minor
       advantage,
Though it is not a passage out of existence.
Ah, that it were, my mother,
Then would we have true marriages!
Rejoicing points our way through the little door at the back of the
       garden,
Hidden in the vine-leaves that we in all our power of thought are
       afraid to part.

To rejoice for death is to mourn existence,

As we do in the vine-covered depths of imagination,

All secretly, all in vestigial instinct unknown to us, as animals who
regard the world with scorn,

Look at them, great panthers, wolves, study those eyes, they hold
our own ancestral, proud resentment,

Existence is the crime against the existing, and no matter who is
the criminal,

(The death of God, like the death of Hitler, is an affair of no
consequence),

This thisness that is, all this something that could just as well be
nothing,

The seed or the sequoia, the neutron or the galaxy,

What is and is and is and is and is,

Oh, in my rage at No One to address, I cry out: Intelligence,

(For mind is implicit in it all),

Give over, it is enough, let existence subside,

All that words point to meaninglessly like vanes jerked in the wind,

Sea, land, sun, consciousness, the universe, most meaningless word
of all (the fantastical converting into one),

I cry out for us all, Desist, give again the void, the one word that
means everything.

3. The Ship

Margery Tracy Barrow Dibb Thummell Sterling Carruth, you used
     to rattle out
Your name like a litany, your Latin that nevertheless remained
     for you a little charm,
You linked, you connected, a place for you in the generations of
     Old England,
Yet you told me nothing of your family, you ran away from home
     when you were sixteen,
A lost child whose kinship was the waifs, those Dickensian forlorn
     whom everyone must love,
And only later did I learn that Tracy was the knight (the punk)
     who inserted the stiletto (the shiv) into Thomas à Becket,
Or that Barrow was rector of Christ Church, tutor to Isaac Newton,
     artificer of much of the *Principia,*
(When first I read what John Aubrey wrote of him, I was as if
     swept gently into an eddy of time by my admiration),
You in the long moment of death remembering your voyage (were
     they two? I think so) to England,
(And now my memory comes clearer, your vessel was the
     Mauretania),
How you crossed the shining water from earth to the great ship,
And went forth on the dark sea,
A child you were,
Then an old woman dying,
An event, an instant.

Clearly the first sailors were the dead. Why do I find here no
      scholars?
(Intelligence a structure of optimism, the human error, and thus
      ships must have carried corporate earnings to Thebes.)
The dead was placed on a dead tree at the riverside and sent on its
      voyage to the sea,
The temple of Osiris was built with a moated pool in the forecourt,
      on which voyaged a toy boat, the Ship of the Dead, wafted
This way and that by the currents of air that were Ra's
      whisperings,
And it is told that such a temple existed in Taunton, Massachusetts,
      which I believe,
For surely I am an Heliopolitan and Isis is my mother, and I dwell
      in the curse of Thoth forever,
(And yet, You Jackal, Eater of Carrion, if words were inevitable
      in your numen, how more wondrously than the
      hieroglyphikos, the priest-writing?),
And all oceans run westward in our minds,
And if rivers appear not to, still we must cross them,
The ferry, shadow of the sun's barque, each sundown into the
      dying aureole,
A lingering, languishing disappearance (appearance in Dis).

I have seen the jet at 35,000 feet, a spark in the sunset, under
      Hesperus, infinitesimal,
And then no more,
The empty acorn cupule, vacancy so vast, turning in the rivulet.
      (Akran, Goth., fruit.)

Has anyone ever set foot aboard without a dark inarticulate
      knowledge of the true cargo?
The little last-minute hesitancy of embarkation.

Mother, I stood on the pier with you, in the turbulence of whirling
      images,
I leaned down to you, down to your words muffled by the wind,
I watched you cross, I waved to you, I smiled and took off my hat,
Little blonde girl frowning at the rail, your muff and shining black
      shoes,
The flowers crushed to your chest.

4. The Phantasmagoria

She shook him and the boy tumbled down the stairs, bouncing
        oddly from side to side. A box containing a loose weight.
At Hartford on the deck of the packet, awaiting departure, they sat
        under an awning and stared at the rainbow, one end of
        which was located in the river halfway to the opposite shore.
The young woman, dressed in a long dark flannel skirt and a blouse
        buttoned at the throat with a wide white collar, held the
        reins with both hands, but lightly, as the carriage lurched
        up Hardscrabble Hill.
The dresser was painted, medium gray enamel, a white cloth with
        cross-stitched hem in blue thread, a large mirror behind,
        speckled in one corner where the silver had flaked. A
        hairbrush, comb, and handmirror of tarnished silver. In the
        middle of the cloth lay her favorite pendant, a blue
        moonstone very delicately carved to reveal the face within.
        Decades later it was presented to a granddaughter and now
        lies at the bottom of the Gulf of California off Isla San
        Marcos.
In the spring of 1926 she ran across a lawn, into an orchard, where
        apple petals fell thickly about her. She wore a short skirt,
        tennis shoes, a sweater, a double strand of amber beads. In
        the brightness her legs flashed whitely.
Her diary. Small black-covered record books, scores of them over
        the decades. She wrote at a carved oval table in the corner
        of the dining room, next to a fern and a telephone. For fifty
        years she used a green Parker pen with a gold loop in the

cap for suspending it on a ribbon, though she never carried it that way.

When her first great-grandchild was born in 1970, she tried to feel glad, but it was useless. She bitched and nagged as usual. No room for great-grandchildren in her vision of the House of Reality.

At age four she stood on a piano stool in a white ruffled dress and played a half-sized violin. The music was not preserved in the photograph. Later one of her favorite recordings—she had many—was Menuhin's performance of the concerto by Mendelssohn.

At seven she dined at Delmonico's and marveled at the ballet girls dancing overhead, their skirts whirling in circles above the glass ceiling.

At thirty-three she went to bed for six months. "Pernicious anemia." It was successful and from time to time thereafter she repeated it.

She and her two friends, Madge and Milicent, canned peaches all day, filling the kitchen with steam. A cloying odor. This was in 1939.

In 1925 she refused to sleep any longer in the same bed with her husband. She kept the white enameled, iron double bedstead for herself. In 1928 she began refusing to accompany him on his Sunday afternoon walks.

When her husband died, week after week she wept for his loss while she watched baseball on the TV. "He was a good man," someone said. "He was the only person who could comfort me in my trials," she answered. It was true.

The assembly of skeletal crones in their wheelchairs near the
    nurses' station. The smell. The inosculation of thecal
    miseries. The wails and babblement. Death permeative.
    Dachau.

Her pride. Never to include the lack of money among her
    complaints. To keep her house orderly and clean; to cover
    up its shabbiness. In old age she implored and cajoled, that
    others might wash the windows.

Her fear of coal gas. How she ran to the cellar door to sniff. How
    she threw up the sashes when someone farted.

Over and over she read the novels of Arnold Bennett, H. G. Wells,
    Helen Hunt Jackson, H. Rider Haggard, W. Somerset
    Maugham, Hugh Walpole, etc. But when television came,
    she gave up reading.

In her first years of marriage she wrote stories for girls and sold
    them to a children's magazine. Then she lost interest. A few
    years later her husband gave up writing poetry, although he
    had enjoyed a modest success in the slicks.

When she was a girl she skated to school from 96th and Central
    Park West to (I believe) 83rd and Amsterdam. Sometimes,
    if the north wind were strong, she could coast the whole
    way.

She delighted in avocados exceedingly, and was put out with her
    family because no one would eat oysters. She regarded her
    marriage as a social, though perhaps not a cultural,
    catastrophe. She ate avocados standing at the kitchen
    cabinet and scraped the hulls with her spoon. She called
    them alligator pears.

Anemia. Miscarriage. Chronic psoriasis. Hemorrhoids. Gallstones.
Chronic cystitis. Uterine cancer. Cataracts. Toothache.
Many cerebral incidents. Rectal cancer. Two major strokes.
When was her finest hour? She does not know. She remembers
only successive faint sensations of imprisonment and flight.

5. The Mother

The Indo-European root *pha*, suggesting light and clarity, surfaces
       in *phenomenon*, the thing that appears,
And also in the Greek for "I say," *phemi*, thence in *phonation*,
       verb, word,
(And, I suspect, in *speech*, though my magic partridge is roosting
       in some other hemlock tonight),
For appearance is nothing until it has been spoken and written,
       nothing at all,
And now words are revenant, like the tides of shards drifting on
       the waste at Old Oraibe,
The issues my friends and I *settled* twenty years ago or thirty
       years ago
Are now impossible even to describe.

Nana, so remote, yet only second in the chain of motherhood,
(My own grandchildren sending crayoned flowers as I sent mine
       to you),
You brushed your waist-long hair until it shone like burnished
       metal, you wore dead foxes with bright little eyes,
You came with trunks and hatboxes and bright packages of toys,
       and you stayed two days, and you departed,
You vanished into the train, which went away calling Who?
       Whoooo?
And you carried a book called *Science and Health*, which you left
       open upon the bed when you flumped from the hotel
       window,

And beyond you is no name, no woman, no mother, far down the
valley of dark wind,
None in the mountain pass, none on the sunlit plain,
Far and far to the grove by the sea where dwells the water-woman
whose beauty is too great to be looked upon
And where the bronzen child calls always in the sea-wind Who?
Whoooo?

And the words are tokens, and the tokens are despair,
And the silence which is beyond everything, the silence which is
around everywhere, is unattainable,
No death can reach it.

Hypocritical reader, you think you know better than I, and you do,
But your knowledge is *tones*, not meanings; it is soothings and
alarms,
The unrolling and rolling up
Of contrivance unending, images, blandishments, the calculus of
inexperience in a thingless world,
The flat screen;
And your knowledge is the massive dictatorship that runs this
camp of ignorance where I find myself;
Oh, the loathing with which I look out upon you, my horror, my
despair.

6. The Son

I held out my fingers while you burnt them with matches, one
       after another,
I snuggled close to you in the deserted railway station in Southbury
       while whirling snow filled the night,
I was astonished when you shrieked because you imagined I would
       marry the woman next door,
I never told you, when you visited me every week during the year
       and a half of my commitment, how grateful I was that you
       brought no other gifts,
I swallowed when you forced the castor oil into my mouth for
       punishment,
I cooked dinner in the fear of mystery when you lay ill and called
       directions to me in your unrecognizable voice,
I ducked when you stroked the back of my head and told me I had
       the handsomest nape in the world,
I tried not to scream when you hit me with my father's strop,
I tried not to cry when you fed me junket and sweet custard with
       the half-sized silver spoon, those times when I had measles
       and rheumatic fever,
I ironed the pillow cases, towels, and handkerchiefs, you ironed the
       shirts and sheets,
I came to you in shame when I pissed in my pants at age twelve
       because I could hold it no longer,
I stared when you held the ether over my nose in a tea strainer so
       the doctor could cut out my tonsils on the dining table,
I wondered when you held my face in your palms and looked at
       me a long, long time until I cast down my eyes,

I was shocked when you laughed delightedly at the hot juice
     fountaining up from the cherry cobbler and spurting all
     over the linen,
I was sobered when you took me to school and explained
     everything to the teacher,
I never understood (how could I?) the hunger of your love, nor why
     you called me selfish . . .

Often people ask me how you were as a mother, and I ask myself
     how I was as a son, but what shall I answer?
We were like no others.
I know this. Anything else is inconceivable. My mind will not
     think it.
But more I cannot say, for what created our difference is still
     unknown to me.

7. The Death

On the sea of motherhood and death you voyaged, waif of eternity,
You were the pioneer whether you knew it or not,
You were the unwitting pioneer, and most of the time unwilling,
You who for seventy years despised your stepfather, I am certain
       (in the nature of things) with justice,
You who knowingly first met your father when you were thirty,
The seedy businessman from St. Louis, that droll city,
You whose husband, loving and incapable, the knight in podgy
       armor, the poet from the land of the Brownies,
Talking away your blues with the wisdom he gave instead of love
       and that he himself could never use,
(Oh, might I say, with the dicky bird, that things past redress are
       now with me past care!),
You, my mother, who taught me without words that no secret is
       better kept than the one everybody guesses,
I see you now in your eternal moment that has become mine,
You twisted, contorted, your agonized bones,
You whom I recognize forever, you in the double exposure,
You in the boat of your confinement lying,
Drifting on the sea as the currents and long winds take you,
Penitent for the crime committed against you, victim of your own
       innocence,
(Existence is the crime against the existing),
Drifting, drifting in the uncaused universe that has no right to be.

Index of Titles and First Lines

New Directions Paperbooks—A Partial Listing

For complete listing request free catalog from
New Directions, 80 Eighth Avenue, New York 10011   †Bilingual

For complete listing request free catalog from
New Directions, 80 Eighth Avenue, New York 10011

†Bilingual